CATS REACT to SCIENCE FACTS

By Izzi Howell

SCHOLASTIC

Library of Congress Cataloging-in-Publication Data

Names: Howell, Izzi, author.
Title: Cats react to science facts/Izzi Howell.
Description: New York: Franklin Watts, an imprint of Scholastic Inc., 2020. | Audience: Grades 7-9. | Summary: "The book is about science facts and how cats react to them"—Provided by publisher.
Identifiers: LCCN 2019036088 | ISBN 9780531235331 (library binding) | ISBN 9780531244425 (paperback) |
Subjects: LCSH: Science—Miscellanea—Juvenile literature. | Children's questions and answers.
Classification: LCC Q163 .H7945 2020 | DDC 502—dc23

Copyright © The Watts Publishing Group, 2019
First published by Franklin Watts 2019
Published in the United States by Scholastic Inc. 2020

Printed in China

SCHOLASTIC, FRANKLIN WATTS, and associated logos are trademarks and/or registered trademarks of Scholastic Inc.

1 2 3 4 5 6 7 8 9 10 R 29 28 27 26 25 24 23 22 21 20

Scholastic Inc., 557 Broadway, New York, NY 10012.

The publisher would like to thank the following for permission to reproduce their pictures:

Getty: ZargonDesign 16t, adogslifephoto 18l, flibustier 21t, LUHUANFENG 22br, gsermek 25t, leonello 27t, bahadir-yeniceri 29, shayes17 31b, normaals 32r, eurobanks 39l and 59br, jarnogz 39r, JanPietruszka 40b and 2, iridi 42, deshy 44t, MirasWonderland 61b, Jawcam 62t, Buffy1982 66b, iridi 68, mikdam 73, Stephen Oliver 74t, anurakpong 74b, RG-vc 77c, spxChrome 77b, phant 79, Roger Ressmeyer/Corbis/VCG 81, GlobalP 84, Dmytro Lastovych 100, ilterriorm 105t.
Shutterstock: Ambartsumian Valery cover, Seregraff, TungCheung, PHOTOCREO Michal Bednarek, CebotariN, Ekaterina Kolomeets back cover t–b, l–r, Clari Massimiliano 4t, Sonsedska Yuliia 4b, 8br, 38, 92 and 95t, DreamBig 5, Computer Earth 6–7, Iryna Kuznetsova 6b, 10b, 18r, 37, 47t, 55t, 59tl, 70l, 83b, 86 ,98, 103b and 107, Asichka 7b, Suzanne Tucker title page, 8t, 8c and 76b, turlakova 8bl, Ozerov

Alexander 10t, Mopic 11t, Ermolaev Alexander 11b, 33b, 34b, 44b and 88b, 3D Vector 12l, Johan Swanepoel 12r, nevodka 13, LanKS 14tl, Baronb 14tr, Designua 14c, sdominick 14bl, Tony Campbell 14br, 17t, 21t, 27b, 59bl and 109b, Aphelleon 15, GrigoryL 15t, 15b and 109t, Sergey Moskvitin 16t, Castleski 16b, yevgeniy11 17b, Suzi44 19l, Rasulov 19r, Utekhina Anna 20l, Peter Hermes Furian 20r, Vilor 21t, Nailia Schwarz 22t, oksana2010 22bl, Dr Morley Read 23t, Sarah Fields Photography 23b,Tatjana Dimitrievska 24, Stav krikst 25b, Eric Isselee 26, 54t, 58l, 60, 68, 69 and 96, tobkatrina 28 and 76t, umnola 29, IMissisHope 30, Andrey_Kuzmin 31t, Okssi 32l, Martina Osmy 33t, Bilevich Olga 34t and 111t, Mr.Nakorn 35t, Lightspring 35b, Kirsanov Valeriy Vladimirovich 36t, WilleeCole Photography 36b, alekss-sp 37, Ewa Studio 40t, 5 second Studio 41t, Ian 2010 41b, Viorel Sima 43t, critterbiz 43b, kuban_girl 45, 48t, 63l and 102, Dixi_ 46t, iagodina 46b, Dora Zett 47bl, chrisbrignell 47br, Yellow Cat 48b, Smiler99 49t, Stefano Garau 49b, Oksana Kuzmina 50tl, Roland Ijdema 50tr, Fernanda Leite 50bl, MirasWonderland 50br, Rasulov 51t, EEI_Tony 51bl, Ivonne Wierink 51br, revers 52t, Oksana Kuzmina 52b, ekkapon 53tl, MaraZe 53tr, Nynke van Holten 53bl, LightField Studios 53br, Craig Walton 54t and 54b, , Seregraff 54t and 64, Kirill Vorobyev, Chirtsova Natalia 54b, cyo bo 55b, canbedone 56t, Tercer Ojo Photography 56b, DK samco 57t, Jurik Peter 57b, MoreenBlackthorne and Vitaly Titov 58r, FotoYakov 59tr, Eivaisla 3 and 61t, Alex Coan 63b, Pixfiction 63rVitoriano Junior 65, Tom Wang 66t, apiguide 67t, Susan Schmitz 67b, Zhao jian kang, Gearstd, mstanley and Lightspring 68, JBArt 69, arrogant 70–71, Alexey Stiop and Natalia Tretiakova 72, Milarka 75t, haryigit 75b, Mark_KA 77t, Robynrg 78, hannadarzy 80t, bmf-foto.de 80b, Nadja Antonova 82t, P.S_2 82b, R. Maximiliane 83T, ANURAK PONGPATIMET 85l, 123object 85r, Le Do, kirillov Alexey, Krisana Antharith, Studio Smart, Cat'chy Images, Manu Padilla 86, showcake 88t, Hayati Kayhan, Andrey Solovev, HolyCrazyLazy 89, Filipe B. Varela 90, dugdax 91t, StudioLondon 91b, Angela Kotsell 93t, Alexander Mazurkevich 93b, atiger 94t, Sergey Katyshkin 94b, Bogdan Wankowicz 95b, Jagodka, Tony Campbell 96, stocknadia, Yuguesh Fagoonee, metha1819 97, Africa Studio 98 and 103t, Sheila Fitzgerald 99, Nerthuz 101t, Andrey_Kuzmin 101b, Ivanova N 104t, PRO Stock Professional 104b, Damsea 105b, PRILL 106l, N-studio 106r, DenisNata 108, nevodka 110, Tuzemka 111b.

Cats React cats from Shutterstock: Lubava, Seregraff, Jagodka and Getty: GlobalP, Arseniy45.

All design elements from Shutterstock.

Every attempt has been made to clear copyright. Should there be any inadvertent omission, please apply to the publisher for rectification.

CONTENTS

SCIENCE IS AMAZING!

Did you know that **HOT WATER** can **FREEZE FASTER** than **COLD WATER?**

Or that it's almost **IMPOSSIBLE** to **BURP IN SPACE** because gas can't separate from food in the stomach without **GRAVITY?**

Discover **MIND-BLOWING SCIENCE FACTS** and **LAUGH** along with these **CRAZY CAT REACTIONS!** Do you **AGREE** with the **REACT-O-METER**?

SCIENTISTS HAVE BEEN ABLE TO CHANGE THE **GENES** OF A CAT TO CREATE **CATS** THAT **GLOW IN THE DARK!**

OMG!

No way!

Gross!

Wow!

Mind-blowing!

THE S🪐LAR SYSTEM

Our solar system is a **COLLECTION OF EIGHT PLANETS** and many other, **SMALLER OBJECTS,** all of which travel around **THE SUN.**

Sun

Mercury

Venus

Earth

Mars

STAR PAWS

THE SUN is at the **CENTER** of the solar system. Its **GRAVITY** pulls the planets into **ORBIT** around it.

Uranus

Neptune

Saturn

Jupiter

There are **HUNDREDS** of **MOONS** in the solar system. Moons orbit **ASTEROIDS** and **PLANETS**, including Earth.

The **PLANETS** are all very **DIFFERENT**.

Neptune is the **MOST DISTANT** planet. It takes 165 EARTH YEARS to orbit the sun!

Jupiter is the **LARGEST** planet. It is **TWICE THE SIZE** of all the other planets in the solar system combined!

Some **CLOUDS** on Uranus smell like **ROTTEN EGGS!**

Venus is the **HOTTEST** planet. Its surface temperature is 869°F, hot enough to **MELT LEAD!**

THE SUN

The sun is a **STAR**—a huge ball of **INCREDIBLY HOT GAS!**

The sun provides **LIGHT** and **HEAT** to **EARTH** and all other planets in our solar system.

Without the sun, there would be

no **LIFE ON EARTH**.

The sun is the **LARGEST** object in the solar system. **ONE MILLION EARTHS** could fit inside it.

EARTH

Earth is the only known **PLANET**
that supports **LIFE**.

Earth has two **IMPORTANT THINGS** that living things
need—**WATER** and an atmosphere filled with **OXYGEN**.
It is the **RIGHT DISTANCE** from the sun so it isn't **TOO
HOT** or **TOO COLD** on the surface.

The inside of Earth
has layers of hot
molten rock.

The surface of Earth
is covered with land
and water.

The hottest part
of Earth is
its core.

I'm feline a bit dizzy!

EARTH IS **CONSTANTLY**

MOVING, ALTHOUGH

WE CAN'T FEEL IT!

It **SPINS ON ITS AXIS** (an imaginary line that runs through the **NORTH** and **SOUTH POLES**) and moves in **ORBIT** around the sun!

OMG!

No way!

Gross!

Wow!

Mind-blowing!

It takes Earth 365¼ **DAYS** to **ORBIT** the sun. Earth is **TILTED**, which means that different parts of the planet are closer to the sun throughout the year. This creates the **SEASONS**.

This diagram shows the seasons for the Northern Hemisphere, the top half of Earth.

spring

winter

The Northern Hemisphere is **TILTED TOWARD** the sun in summer.

The Northern Hemisphere is **TILTED AWAY** from the sun in winter.

summer

autumn

THE MOON

The moon is the only **NATURAL SATELLITE** that **ORBITS EARTH.**

The moon appears to **SHINE** in the **NIGHT SKY.** However, it isn't producing its own light.

It's **REFLECTING LIGHT** from the sun.

The moon is the only body in space that **HUMANS HAVE VISITED.** People first set foot on the moon in **1969.**

LIGHT SOURCES

Some human-made light sources, such as lamps, are powered by **ELECTRICITY.**

Light sources are things that **GIVE OFF LIGHT.**

The sun creates almost all of the **NATURAL LIGHT** on Earth. We often use human-made sources of light inside or at night.

I love furry tails!

PUSS IN BOOTS

FIRE is a light source we use with **CANDLES.**

ANGLERFISH CAN MAKE THEIR OWN LIGHT! THEIR LIGHT ATTRACTS OTHER ANIMALS, WHICH THE ANGLERFISH ATTACKS AND EATS!

Wow! No way! OMG! Gross! Mind-blowing!

THE EYE

We **SEE OBJECTS** when **LIGHT REFLECTS** off them and travels into the eye.

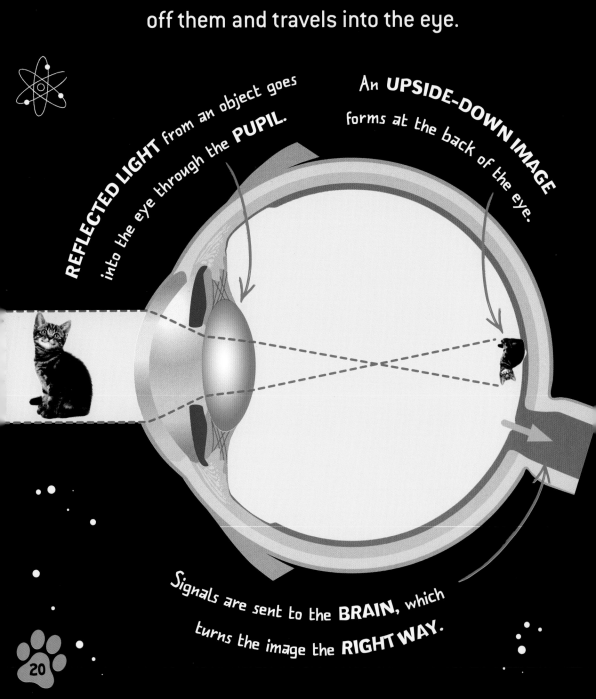

REFLECTED LIGHT from an object goes into the eye through the **PUPIL.**

An **UPSIDE-DOWN IMAGE** forms at the back of the eye.

Signals are sent to the **BRAIN**, which turns the image the **RIGHT WAY**.

SOME **ANIMALS** CAN SEE **LIGHT** THAT **HUMANS** CAN'T. **BEES** ARE ATTRACTED TO **INVISIBLE LIGHT PATTERNS** ON FLOWERS, WHICH GUIDE THEM TOWARD **SWEET NECTAR!**

OMG!

No way!

Gross!

Wow!

Mind-blowing!

MOVING THROUGH MATERIALS

>>>>>> LIGHT can pass through some MATERIALS. >>>>>>

TRANSPARENT MATERIALS, such as glass, let light through. You can see perfectly through them.

OPAQUE MATERIALS don't let any light through. You can't see through them.

TRANSLUCENT MATERIALS let some light through. You can see some details through them.

Is my lunch in there?

THE UNDERSIDE OF THE GLASS FROG FROM SOUTH AMERICA IS TRANSPARENT— YOU CAN SEE ITS INTERNAL ORGANS!

No way!

OMG!

Gross!

Wow!

Mind-blowing!

SHADOWS

SHADOWS are
formed when an object
BLOCKS LIGHT.

When a translucent or opaque object **BLOCKS LIGHT**, it creates
AN AREA OF DARKNESS (shadow) behind the object.
The size and shape of the shadow depend on the
POSITION and size of the light source.

THOUSANDS OF YEARS AGO, PEOPLE TOLD THE TIME USING SHADOWS! ON A SUNDIAL, THE SHADOW LINES UP WITH THE TIME.

The purrfect alarm clock!

Wow! No way! OMG! Gross! Mind-blowing!

REFLECTION

When **LIGHT RAYS** hit an object, they are **ABSORBED** or **REFLECTED**.

DARK OBJECTS absorb almost all light.
NO REFLECTION can be seen.

SMOOTH, SHINY OBJECTS reflect almost all light. The reflection is **VERY CLEAR**.

Mirror, mirror on the wall, who's the furriest of them all?

LIGHT RAYS CAN **BEND** WHEN THEY MOVE FROM ONE MATERIAL TO ANOTHER. THAT'S WHY IT LOOKS LIKE THE **TOP** OF THE PENCIL IS IN A DIFFERENT POSITION FROM THE **BOTTOM.**

No way!

OMG!

Gross!

Wow!

Mind-blowing!

SOUND WAVES

SOUND WAVES are made when **OBJECTS VIBRATE**.

sound waves are **INVISIBLE**. They can travel through **SOLIDS, LIQUIDS, AND GASES**.

I know you can hear me!

SLOW VIBRATIONS make low-pitched sounds.

QUICK VIBRATIONS make high-pitched sounds.

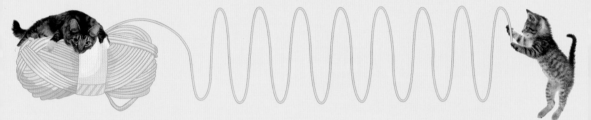

STRONG VIBRATIONS make loud sounds.

WEAK VIBRATIONS make quiet sounds.

THE **LOUDEST KNOWN SOUND** EVER WAS THE **ERUPTION OF THE KRAKATOA VOLCANO** IN INDONESIA IN 1883. PEOPLE HEARD THE SOUND **2,200 MI** AWAY IN AUSTRALIA!

OMG!

No way!

Gross!

Wow!

Mind-blowing!

THE EAR

EARS pick up SOUND WAVES from the AIR.

1 The outer ear has a CURVED SHAPE, which funnels sound waves into the ear.

2 Sound waves travel inside the ear and make the EARDRUM VIBRATE.

outer ear

middle ear

eardrum

MEOW!

inner ear

3 The vibrations travel through the MIDDLE EAR and the INNER EAR.

4 Nerves in the inner ear send signals to the BRAIN, which understands them as sounds.

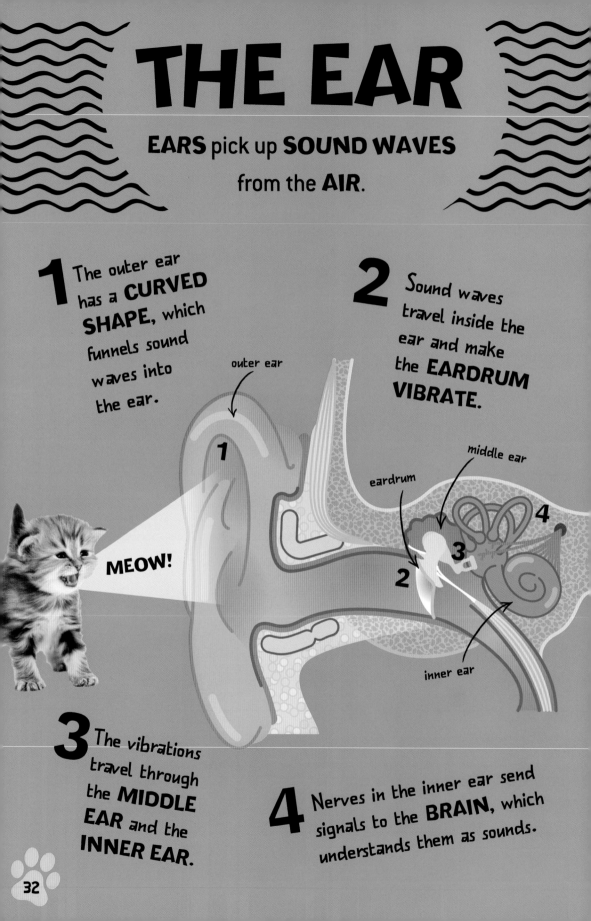

ANIMAL HEARING

Some ANIMALS have much BETTER HEARING than HUMANS DO!

Animals such as cats and dogs can hear **MUCH HIGHER SOUNDS** than humans can.

Their **LARGE, CURVED EARS** help them pick up quiet sounds.

Too close!

Animals move their ears toward a sound so they can hear it better.

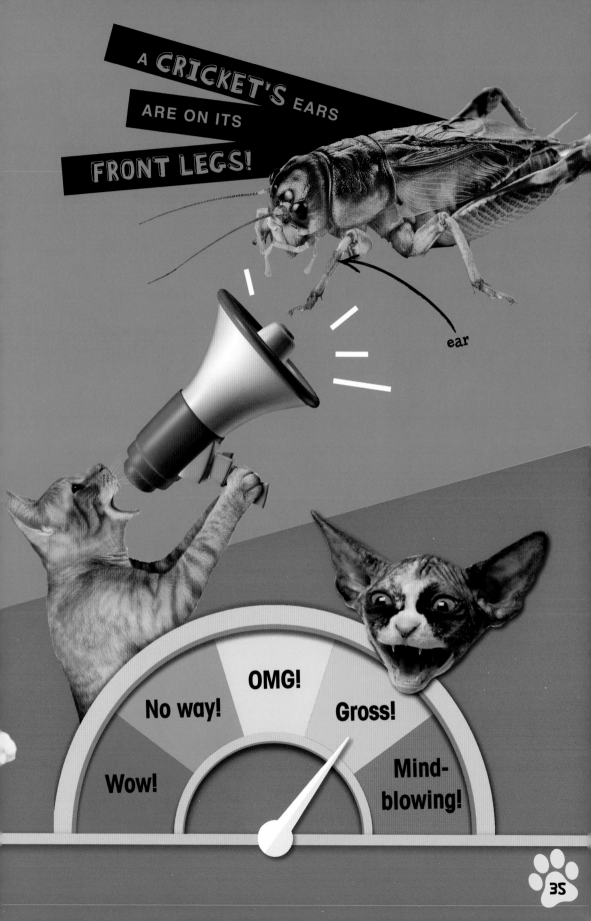

A **CRICKET'S** EARS ARE ON ITS **FRONT LEGS!**

ear

Wow! No way! OMG! Gross! Mind-blowing!

35

Some animals use sound to NAVIGATE and HUNT when they can't see well. They make sounds that BOUNCE OFF OBJECTS around them and echo back.

The animals use these ECHOES to find their way through their surroundings. This is known as ECHOLOCATION.

BATS use echolocation to hunt for food and navigate IN THE DARK.

Help! I'm friend, not food!

DOLPHINS use echolocation to find fish and navigate IN MURKY WATER.

Go find me a fishy!

Dolphins COMMUNICATE with each other using WHISTLES and CLICKING SOUNDS. Some have their OWN SPECIAL whistle sound that they use to IDENTIFY themselves, like a NAME.

MAKING MUSIC

When we play a **MUSICAL INSTRUMENT**, it creates **VIBRATIONS**, which are then heard as **SOUND**.

PERCUSSION INSTRUMENTS make sound when they are hit. The force of the hit makes the instrument vibrate, which creates sound.

STRING INSTRUMENTS make sound when their strings vibrate. The strings of a string instrument can be plucked, strummed, or played with a bow.

When a musician blows into a **WIND INSTRUMENT**, it makes the air inside vibrate. This creates sound.

FUR FiGHTERS

SOME **PIPE ORGANS** CAN PLAY NOTES WITH SUCH A **LOW PITCH** THAT **HUMANS** **CAN'T HEAR** **THEM!**

No way!

OMG!

Gross!

Wow!

Mind-blowing!

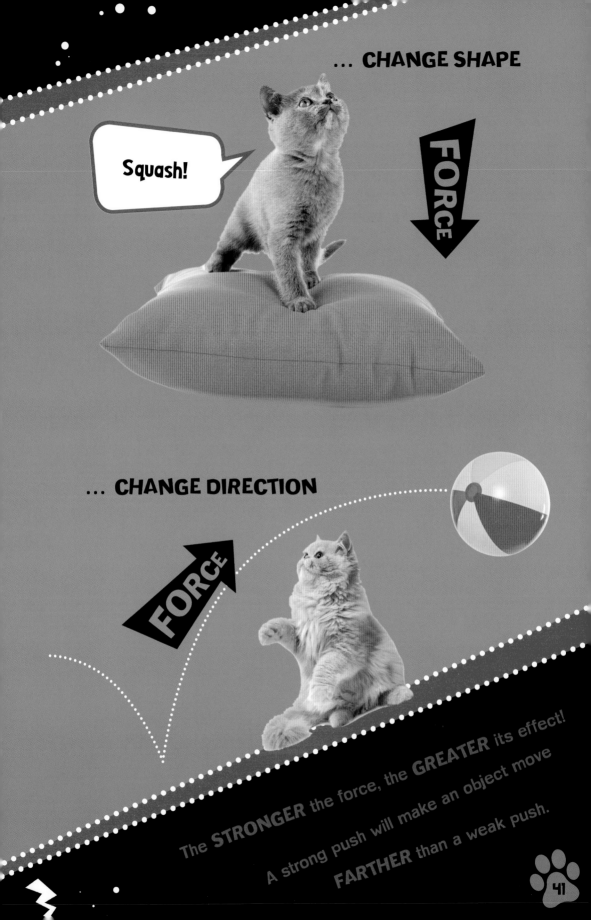

Some objects need to **TOUCH** for forces to have

an effect. Other forces, such as **GRAVITY** and

MAGNETIC FORCE (see pages 44–45 and 52–57),

can happen at a **DISTANCE**.

THE BALL WON'T
MOVE UNTIL IT IS PUSHED
BY THE FOOT.

The body can produce strong forces. Every time you throw, push, or hit something, you are applying force to it.

Eeek!

A GRIZZLY BEAR'S BITE HAS SO MUCH FORCE THAT IT CAN CRUSH A BOWLING BALL!

GRAVITY

GRAVITY is a force that pulls things **TOWARD EACH OTHER.**

On **EARTH**, gravity pulls objects toward the center of the planet.

That means that they **FALL TO THE GROUND.**

Stupid gravity!

Gravity also keeps Earth and other planets in **ORBIT AROUND THE SUN.**

PANCAKES ARE ALWAYS ROUND BECAUSE OF GRAVITY! GRAVITY PULLS DOWN ON THE BATTER EVENLY, STRETCHING THE PANCAKE INTO A CIRCULAR SHAPE!

Break-fur-st is ready!

Wow!
No way!
OMG!
Gross!
Mind-blowing!

FRICTION

FRICTION is a force that acts on an object moving **ACROSS A SURFACE**.

Friction works in the **OPPOSITE DIRECTION** of the moving object and **SLOWS IT DOWN**.

The **ROUGHER** the surface, the **MORE FRICTION** there will be and the **SLOWER** the object will move.

ICE is very **SMOOTH**, and so it causes **LITTLE FRICTION**. It's easy to **SLIP**, unless you are wearing shoes with **ROUGH SOLES** that create friction.

Puss in boots isn't just a fashion statement!

FRICTION wears away **ROCKS** and **SOIL** through a process called **EROSION**. When **WATER, WIND,** or other **ROCKS** rub against the land, they slowly **BREAK IT DOWN** and it **CRUMBLES AWAY.**

LARGE AMOUNTS OF FRICTION CREATE HEAT. WHEN PLANTS OR ROCKS RUB AGAINST EACH OTHER REPEATEDLY, THE HEAT CAUSED BY THE FRICTION CAN SOMETIMES START FOREST FIRES!

RESISTANCE

RESISTANCE is friction acting on objects that are **MOVING THROUGH AIR OR WATER**.

When an object moves through **AIR OR WATER**, friction **SLOWS** it down.

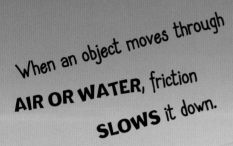

FRICTION

FRICTION

Many objects that travel through air or water have **STREAMLINED (SMOOTH AND SLIM) SHAPES.** This **REDUCES FRICTION** and allows them to move quickly.

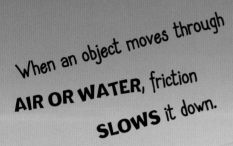

THE **PEREGRINE FALCON** PULLS IN ITS WINGS WHEN IT DIVES TO CATCH PREY. ITS STREAMLINED SHAPE ALLOWS IT TO MOVE AT OVER 200 MPH, WHICH IS AS FAST AS A FORMULA 1 CAR!

No way!

OMG!

Gross!

Wow!

Mind-blowing!

BALANCING FORCES

Forces can be **BALANCED** or **UNBALANCED**.

BALANCED FORCES are two forces of the **SAME SIZE** working on an object in opposite directions. Balanced

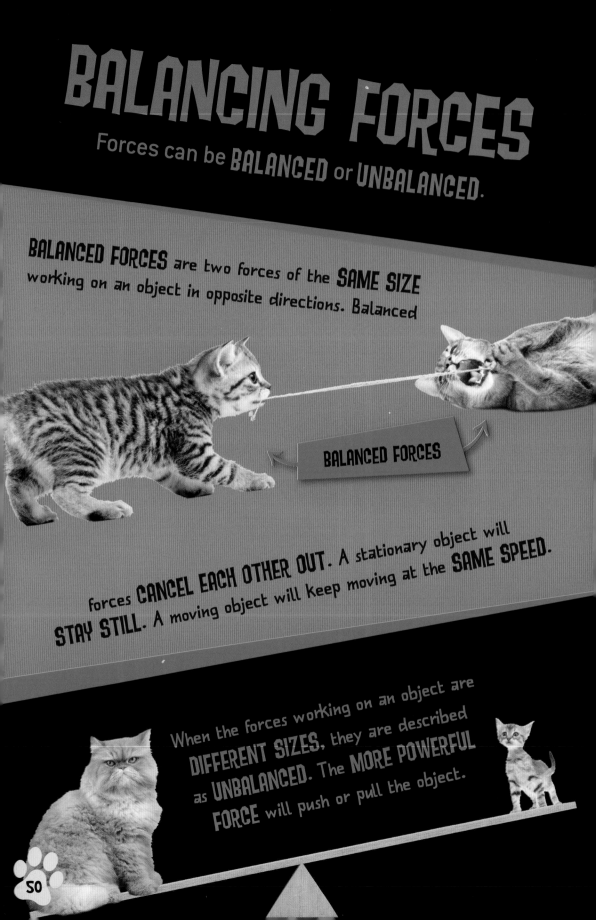

BALANCED FORCES

forces **CANCEL EACH OTHER OUT**. A stationary object will **STAY STILL**. A moving object will keep moving at the **SAME SPEED**.

When the forces working on an object are **DIFFERENT SIZES**, they are described as **UNBALANCED**. The **MORE POWERFUL FORCE** will push or pull the object.

THE POWER OF MAGNETS

A **MAGNET** is an object that **ATTRACTS MAGNETIC MATERIALS**.

The **MAGNETIC FORCE** of a magnet attracts magnetic objects. Some metals, including **IRON** and **NICKEL**, are magnetic.

Paper clips are made of **STEEL**, which is a magnetic material.

Why aren't mice magnetic?!

PLASTIC

GLASS

Plastic, glass, wood, and gold are **NOT MAGNETIC**.

WOOD

GOLD

53

The two ends of a magnet are called the **NORTH POLE** and the **SOUTH POLE**. The south pole of one magnet **ATTRACTS** the north pole of another magnet. Two of the same poles **REPEL** each other.

High five!

Go away!

THE MAGNETIC EARTH

EARTH is a MAGNET.

Earth's magnetic force comes from **ITS CORE**, which is made up of magnetic **IRON AND NICKEL**. It has a magnetic north pole and a magnetic south pole.

COMPASSES use Earth's magnetic field for **NAVIGATION**. North on a compass points to **EARTH'S MAGNETIC NORTH POLE**.

Compass, which way to Fur-rance?

Earth isn't the only **MAGNETIC BODY** in **SPACE**.

MAGNETARS are extremely powerful magnetic stars.

ONE MAGNETAR HAS THE
SAME MAGNETIC STRENGTH
AS ONE HUNDRED
THOUSAND TRILLION
FRIDGE MAGNETS!

OMG!

No way!

Gross!

Wow!

Mind-blowing!

WHAT IS ENERGY?

ENERGY makes things **WORK**.

Every **ACTION** requires **ENERGY**. **LIVING THINGS, MACHINES,** and **VEHICLES** all need energy to move and carry out different actions.

There are many different types of energy.

ELECTRICAL ENERGY

HEAT ENERGY

YELLING FOR 8 YEARS, 7 MONTHS, AND 6 DAYS WOULD PRODUCE ENOUGH ENERGY TO HEAT A CUP OF COFFEE!

One cat-puccino please!

No way!
OMG!
Wow!
Gross!
Mind-blowing!

FOSSIL FUELS

Coal, oil, and natural gas
are fossil fuels.

Coal, oil, and natural gas form **UNDER EARTH'S SURFACE** over **MILLIONS OF YEARS** from the **REMAINS OF PLANTS AND ANIMALS.**

Fossil fuels are a **NONRENEWABLE** resource because they take so **LONG TO FORM.** Once we use up our supply of fossil fuels, we **CAN'T PRODUCE** any more.

Fossil fuels are burned to produce heat and to generate electricity. (see page **70**.)

I love fur-ssil fuels!

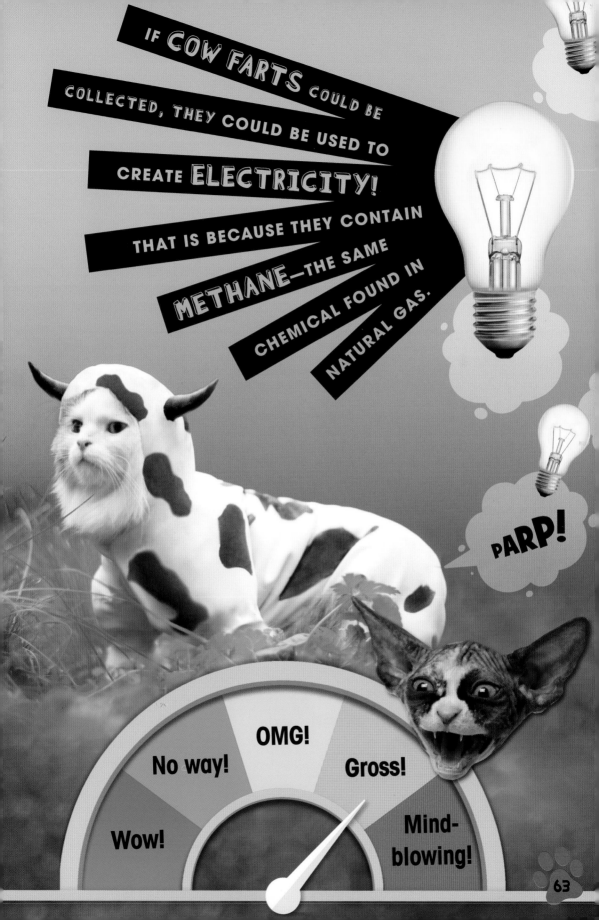

IF **COW FARTS** COULD BE COLLECTED, THEY COULD BE USED TO CREATE **ELECTRICITY!** THAT IS BECAUSE THEY CONTAIN **METHANE**—THE SAME CHEMICAL FOUND IN NATURAL GAS.

PARP!

OMG!

No way!

Gross!

Wow!

Mind-blowing!

63

GLOBAL WARMING

Experts say **BURNING FOSSIL FUELS** leads to **GLOBAL WARMING.**

light (heat) from the sun

When fossil fuels are **BURNED**, gases such as **CARBON DIOXIDE** are released. These gases gather in the **ATMOSPHERE** and trap **LIGHT FROM THE SUN** close to Earth's surface.

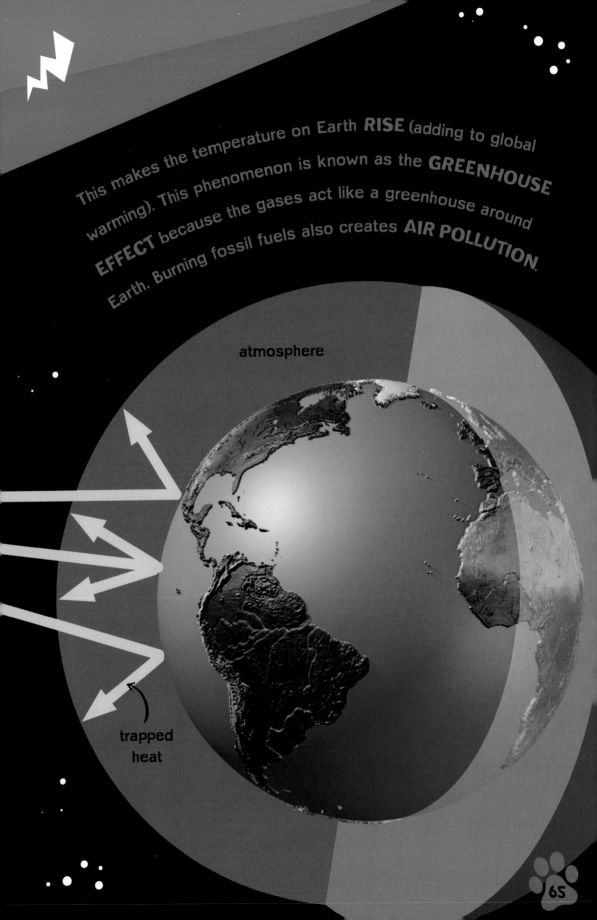

This makes the temperature on Earth **RISE** (adding to global warming). This phenomenon is known as the **GREENHOUSE EFFECT** because the gases act like a greenhouse around Earth. Burning fossil fuels also creates **AIR POLLUTION**.

atmosphere

trapped heat

Global warming and pollution are affecting **ALL LIFE** on Earth. **HABITATS** are being **DESTROYED,** and **PLANT** and **ANIMAL** species are **AT RISK.**

Global warming is a-paw-ling!

GLOBAL WARMING IS TURNING

99% OF SEA TURTLE

EGGS FEMALE IN SOME

PARTS OF AUSTRALIA!

FEMALE TURTLES ARE

MORE LIKELY TO

HATCH IN WARM SAND.

Happy birthday!

OMG!

No way!

Gross!

Wow!

Mind-blowing!

GREEN ENERGY

SOLAR, WIND, and HYDROELECTRIC POWER are good for the environment.

Unlike burning fossil fuels, GENERATING ELECTRICITY from SOLAR PANELS, WIND TURBINES, and HYDROELECTRIC DAMS does NOT release greenhouse gases. It doesn't CREATE AIR POLLUTION either.

No more fur-ssil fuels!

The sun, wind, and water are all RENEWABLE resources. They will never be used up, so we can use them to GENERATE ELECTRICITY FOREVER.

THE AMOUNT OF SUNLIGHT THAT HITS EARTH IN ONE HOUR IS ENOUGH TO POWER THE ENTIRE PLANET FOR A YEAR!

No way!

OMG!

Gross!

Wow!

Mind-blowing!

GENERATING ELECTRICITY

Turbines are used to **GENERATE ELECTRICITY** from **FOSSIL FUELS, WIND,** and **MOVING WATER**.

In **FOSSIL FUEL POWER PLANTS,** fossil fuels are burned to produce heat.

This heat is used to **BOIL WATER,** which produces **STEAM**.

The steam makes a turbine spin, which powers an **ELECTRICITY GENERATOR.**

GIANT TURBINE

In wind turbines and hydroelectric dams, **WIND AND MOVING WATER** power the turbines and generators.

I can see fur miles!

WIND TURBINES can only produce **ELECTRICITY** when it is **WINDY.** Places that depend on wind energy **STORE EXTRA ELECTRICITY** during windy periods so that their supply does not run out.

Don't waste one of your nine lives!

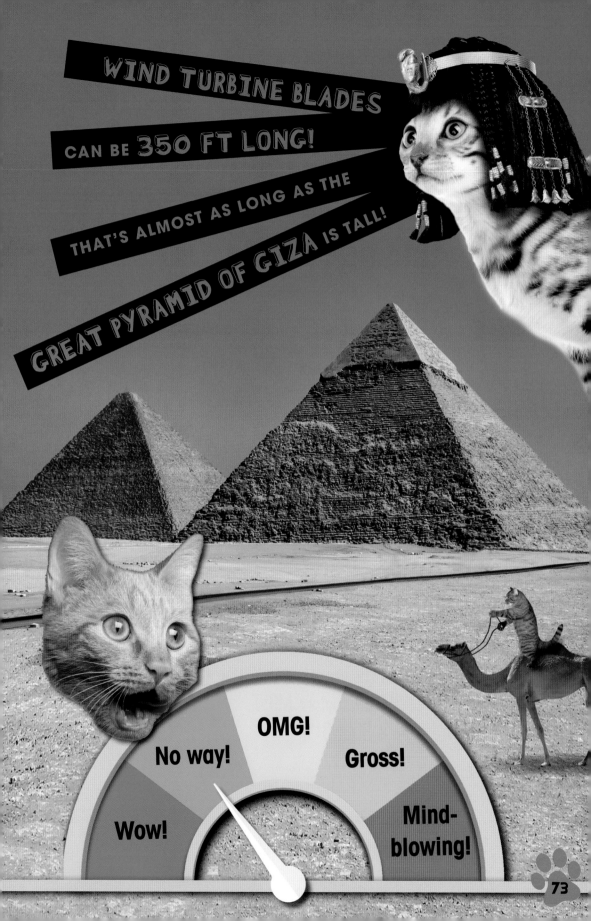

WIND TURBINE BLADES CAN BE **350 FT LONG!**

THAT'S ALMOST AS LONG AS THE GREAT PYRAMID OF GIZA IS TALL!

No way!

OMG!

Gross!

Wow!

Mind-blowing!

CIRCUITS

ELECTRICITY flows around CIRCUITS.

A CIRCUIT is made up of WIRES and a POWER SOURCE, such as a cell or a battery. It can also contain COMPONENTS, such as bulbs, motors, or buzzers.

wire

cell

bulb

Electricity will only travel around COMPLETE CIRCUITS with no gaps in them. When a circuit is complete, electricity POWERS the components in the circuit. Bulbs LIGHT UP, motors MOVE, and buzzers make a SOUND.

Oh, sorry, did you want these wires too?

A **SWITCH** can be used to turn a circuit **ON AND OFF.** When the switch is **CLOSED,** the circuit is **COMPLETE** and electricity flows around it. When the switch is **OPEN,** the circuit is **BROKEN** and the flow of electricity stops.

Light, please!

The electrical power in this circuit is shared between the two bulbs.

SYMBOLS are used to represent the **DIFFERENT PARTS** of a circuit.

switch	→○—○
bulb	→⊗
cell	→┤├
buzzer	→⊓
motor	→Ⓜ
wire	→—

These **SYMBOLS** can be used to **DRAW A DIAGRAM** of a circuit.

This circuit contains a cell, a switch, and a bulb.

Circuit

bulb

switch

cell

LEMONS CAN BE TURNED INTO BATTERIES! WHEN COPPER AND ZINC METALS ARE PLACED IN A LEMON AND CONNECTED BY WIRES, A REACTION TAKES PLACE THAT GENERATES ELECTRICITY.

No way!

OMG!

Gross!

Wow!

Mind-blowing!

ELECTRICITY AND MATERIALS

ELECTRICITY can pass ONLY through SOME MATERIALS.

Materials that electricity can pass through are called CONDUCTORS. Most METALS are conductors, including COPPER, IRON, and STEEL.

INSULATORS are materials that electricity can't pass through. PLASTIC, WOOD, and GLASS are all insulators.

Keep wires away from your cat!

Electrical wires are wrapped in plastic (an insulator) so that the electricity does not escape.

PURIFIED WATER IS AN INSULATOR, BUT TAP WATER IS A CONDUCTOR! THAT IS BECAUSE TAP WATER CONTAINS TINY PARTICLES OF OTHER SUBSTANCES THAT HELP CONDUCT ELECTRICITY.

A refreshing drink *and* a conductor!

STATIC ELECTRICITY

STATIC ELECTRICITY
can form when
INSULATORS
RUB together.

When insulators rub together, **ELECTRONS** (tiny particles with an electrical charge) **JUMP** from one material to the other.

One material **LOSES** its electrical charge, and the other **GAINS** a static electrical charge.

Materials with **OPPOSITE** **CHARGES** are attracted to each other.

If you rub a **BALLOON** on **HAIR**, the hair gains a positive charge and the balloon gains a negative charge. That is why the balloon and the hair **STICK TOGETHER**.

Um, excuse me?!

STATIC ELECTRICITY IS USED IN PRINTERS TO MAKE THE INK STICK TO THE PAPER!

I'm paw-fully photogenic!

No way! OMG! Gross!

Wow! Mind-blowing!

NATURAL ELECTRICITY

ELECTRICITY is generated by ANIMALS and in NATURE.

ALL ANIMALS, including HUMANS, generate small amounts of electricity. This electricity travels through the body along NERVES, carrying messages to and from the BRAIN.

Some animals, however, can generate HUGE AMOUNTS of electricity. The ELECTRIC EEL SHOCKS and KILLS ITS PREY with large bursts of electricity.

Fry me up another fish!

LIGHTNING is a type of NATURAL ELECTRICITY. It builds up in CLOUDS and is released down to the ground.

A BOLT OF LIGHTNING CONTAINS ENOUGH ENERGY TO TOAST 160,000 PIECES OF BREAD!

That's enough break-fur-st for 438 years!

No way!

OMG!

Gross!

Wow!

Mind-blowing!

PLANTS

PLANTS are **LIVING THINGS,**
like animals and humans!

Plants come in many shapes and sizes, from
TINY FLOWERS to **HUGE TREES.** They can
be divided into two groups—**FLOWERING**
and **NONFLOWERING.** Most plants
have flowers (see pages 92-95).

Can you spot
the im-puss-ter?

Most plants live in **SOIL** on **LAND**.
Some plants, such as sea grasses,
live **IN WATER**.

CATCUS

Most plants have **THREE MAIN PARTS:**

LEAVES, ROOTS, and a **STEM.**

The leaves help
make food
for the plant
(see pages 90–91).

The stem supports
the plant.

The roots absorb water and
nutrients from the soil.

CARNIVOROUS PLANTS

GET SOME OF THEIR

NUTRIENTS BY

EATING INSECTS

AND OTHER SMALL

ANIMALS!

These plants live in areas where they can't get all the nutrients they need from the soil.

Run fur your life!

Wow!

No way!

OMG!

Gross!

Mind-blowing!

PHOTOSYNTHESIS

Plants **MAKE ENERGY** using a process called **PHOTOSYNTHESIS.**

Unlike other living things, plants **DON'T EAT FOOD** for energy.

Instead, they **MAKE THEIR OWN ENERGY** using **SUNLIGHT, WATER,** and **CARBON DIOXIDE.**

Plants create oxygen during photosynthesis. Oxygen is released through the leaves.

The leaves trap sunlight and absorb carbon dioxide from the air.

The roots absorb water from the soil.

FLOWERS AND SEEDS

FLOWERS and **SEEDS** are part of a plant's **LIFE CYCLE.**

Flowers contain **POLLEN.** Plants need pollen from other plants of the same species to **PRODUCE SEEDS.** Insects, animals, and the wind **TRANSPORT POLLEN** between plants. This is called **POLLINATION.**

Insects are **ATTRACTED** to **FLOWERS** with a **STRONG SMELL** and **BRIGHTLY COLORED PETALS.**

When insects land on flowers, pollen sticks to their bodies.

THE FLOWERS OF THE RAFFLESIA PLANT SMELL LIKE ROTTING MEAT! THIS ATTRACTS INSECTS THAT HELP POLLINATE THE PLANT.

No way!

OMG!

Gross!

Wow!

Mind-blowing!

After a flower has been pollinated, the **FLOWER DIES AWAY** and **FRUIT GROWS** in its place.

There are **SEEDS** inside the fruit.

This watermelon flower has been pollinated, and a watermelon fruit is growing in its place.

Re-fur-shing!

Seeds are **SCATTERED BY THE WIND** and by

ANIMALS so they aren't too close to the

original plant. **NEW PLANTS** grow

from the seeds.

The process of a seed sprouting and growing

roots is called **GERMINATION**.

SOLIDS

Materials such as **WOOD, PLASTIC,** and **METAL** are **SOLIDS.**

Solid materials have a **FIXED SHAPE.** They **DON'T CHANGE SHAPE** unless a force is applied to them, such as bending, squeezing, or folding.

We're solid, but we can bend and stretch!

Solids always take up the **SAME AMOUNT OF SPACE** and do not spread out unless a **FORCE** is applied.

ROAR!

OSMIUM IS THE HEAVIEST SOLID MATERIAL ON EARTH. 35 CUBIC FT OF OSMIUM WEIGHS 49,800 LB, WHICH IS THE SAME AS TWO AND A HALF TYRANNOSAURUS REXES!

OMG!

No way!

Gross!

Wow!

Mind-blowing!

LIQUID

WATER, MILK, and OIL are all LIQUIDS.

Liquids CHANGE SHAPE to fill the shape of any container that they are in.

They FLOW and CAN BE POURED.

Liquids always take up the SAME AMOUNT OF SPACE.

TAR IS ONE OF THE SLOWEST-MOVING LIQUIDS IN THE WORLD! IT TAKES SEVEN TO THIRTEEN YEARS FOR ONE DROP OF TAR TO FORM!

Too slow!

OMG!

No way!

Gross!

Wow!

Mind-blowing!

GASES

The **AIR** around us is made up of **GASES.**

Gases can **MOVE AROUND FREELY** in the air. If a container filled with gas is left open, the gas will **FLOAT OUT** and escape.

Gases can **EXPAND OR SHRINK** to fit any container, so the amount of space they take up can change.

When you blow up a balloon, gas from your breath spreads out to fill the space inside the balloon.

JUPITER LOOKS SOLID, BUT IT'S ACTUALLY MADE MAINLY OF GAS! IT HAS A SMALL SOLID CORE UNDER THICK LAYERS OF GAS AND LIQUID.

I mew something smelled funny around here!

OMG!

No way!

Gross!

Wow!

Mind-blowing!

CHANGING STATES

Solids, liquids, and gases **CHANGE STATES** when they **CHANGE TEMPERATURE.**

When a liquid falls below a certain temperature, it **FREEZES** into a solid. Different materials melt and freeze at **DIFFERENT TEMPERATURES.**

When the temperature of water falls **BELOW 32°F,** it freezes into **ICE AND SNOW.** If ice is heated to **ABOVE 32°F,** it melts into **WATER.**

When a solid is HEATED, it changes into a liquid. This is called MELTING.

Butter melts when it is heated.

It's a cat-tastrophe!

MELTING ICE CAPS, CAUSED BY GLOBAL WARMING, ARE MAKING SEA LEVELS RISE 1/8 IN EVERY YEAR!

When a **LIQUID** is heated to its **BOILING POINT,** it starts to **BUBBLE** and turn into a gas. Liquids also turn into gases **VERY SLOWLY** when they are left in a **WARM** or **SUNNY PLACE.** This is called **EVAPORATION.**

Wet laundry dries because water evaporates from the clothes.

When the **TEMPERATURE** of a **GAS** drops **BELOW A CERTAIN POINT,** it turns into a **LIQUID.** This is called **CONDENSATION.**

You can often see condensation on windows in cold weather. When water vapor in the air hits the warm window, the vapor condenses into water.

A JELLYFISH IS MADE UP OF 85 TO 98% WATER. WHEN A JELLYFISH WASHES UP ON LAND, NEARLY ALL OF ITS BODY EVAPORATES. IT ALMOST DISAPPEARS ENTIRELY!

OMG!

No way!

Gross!

Wow!

Mind-blowing!

BACK AND FORTH

Some changes of state are **REVERSIBLE.**
Others can never be **REVERSED!**

A **REVERSIBLE CHANGE** makes a material **LOOK** or **FEEL DIFFERENT.** It doesn't create new materials. **MELTING, FREEZING, BOILING,** and **CONDENSING** are all reversible changes.

IRREVERSIBLE CHANGES can create **NEW MATERIALS.** These new materials can't be turned back into the original materials.

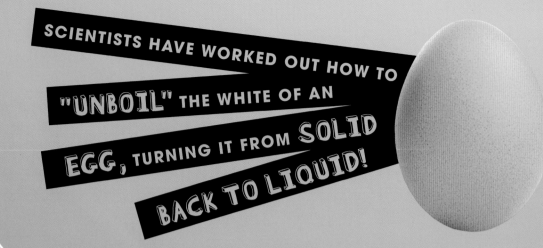

SCIENTISTS HAVE WORKED OUT HOW TO "UNBOIL" THE WHITE OF AN EGG, TURNING IT FROM SOLID BACK TO LIQUID!

However, this process is **SO COMPLICATED** that cooking eggs should still be considered **AN IRREVERSIBLE CHANGE.**

How about break-fur-st after all that science?!

When wood is burned, it turns into smoke and ash. These materials can't be turned back into wood.

107

CLAW-SSARY

asteroid - a space rock that orbits the sun

atmosphere - the gases that surround Earth and other planets

axis - an imaginary line that goes through the center of an object

carbon dioxide - a gas that is released by burning fossil fuels or when humans breathe out

circuit - a system containing wires, batteries, and components

condensation - when gases cool down and turn into liquids

conductor - a material that electricity can pass through

core - the central part of something

eardrum - a thin membrane inside the ear

echo - a sound that is heard after it has bounced off a surface

echolocation - a method of using echoes to hunt or navigate

erosion - when soil and rock are gradually broken down over time by wind or water

evaporation - when liquids heat up and turn into gases

fossil fuels - resources such as coal, oil, and natural gas that form over millions of years and are burned as fuel

freeze - to cool down and turn from a liquid into a solid

friction - a force that acts on an object moving across a surface

gas - a substance that has a form like air and can move freely around

global warming - the increase in temperature on Earth

gravity - a force that pulls things toward each other

greenhouse effect - an effect caused when excess carbon dioxide and other gases gather in Earth's atmosphere, trapping light (heat) from the sun close to Earth's surface

hemisphere - one half of Earth

insulator - a material that electricity can't pass through

irreversible - describes a change that is impossible to undo

liquid - a substance that can flow and take the shape of a container

melt - to heat and turn from a solid into a liquid

molecule - two or more atoms (tiny particles) joined together

molten - in a liquid state

navigate - to find the right direction to travel in

nonrenewable - describes a resource that will eventually run out

nutrient - a substance that an animal or a plant needs to live and grow

opaque - describes something that does not let light pass through, so you can't see through it

orbit - to travel around a planet or a star in a curved path

oxygen - a gas that humans need to breathe to survive

photosynthesis - the process by which plants make energy

pitch - how high or low a sound is

pollination - the process in which pollen is taken from one plant to another so that new seeds can be produced

pupil - the black part of the eye that lets in light

renewable - describes a resource that will never run out

repel - to force something to move away

resistance - friction that works on objects moving through air or water

reversible - describes a change that can be undone

solid - a substance with a fixed shape that always takes up the same amount of space

static electricity - a type of electricity formed when insulators rub together

streamlined - designed in a way that makes it easier to move through air or water

translucent - describes something that lets some light pass through, so you can see some details through it

transparent - describes something that lets light pass through, so you can see through it

turbine - a type of machine in which liquids or gases power a wheel that generates electricity

vibrate - to move back and forth or side to side quickly

FUR-THER INFORMATION

BOOKS

Crazy Plants
by Karina Hamalainen (Scholastic, 2019)

Earth
by Cody Crane (Scholastic, 2018)

Light
by Cody Crane (Scholastic, 2019)

Matter
by Cody Crane (Scholastic, 2019)

The Stars
by Cody Crane (Scholastic, 2018)

You Wouldn't Want to Live Without Gravity!
by Anne Rooney (Scholastic, 2016)

You Wouldn't Want to Live Without Trees!
by Jim Pipe (Scholastic, 2016)

KITTEN-DEX